Celebrate
Christmas

Deborah Heiligman
Consultant, The Reverend Nathan Humphrey

NATIONAL GEOGRAPHIC
WASHINGTON, D.C.

Eric Bleakney reads a Christmas story to his son Ethan at their home in Keystone, Colorado.

carols

∧ *A Christmas present*

On December 25th, Christian people all over the world celebrate Christmas. We celebrate with carols and presents, with prayers and thoughts of peace.

presents

∧ *A dove, symbol of peace*

We celebrate the birth of Jesus Christ, the Son of God. We celebrate his light.

We also celebrate the light of the sun in the middle of a dark, cold winter. We celebrate the warmth of family and friends.

peace

Long, long ago, before Jesus Christ was born, people celebrated the shortest day of the year, the winter solstice, around December 21st. They lit bonfires and candles to coax back the sun. We still light candles at this time of year.

Later, leaders of the Christian church wanted to celebrate the birth of Jesus. They did not know for sure when he was born. But they thought it would be good to celebrate near the winter solstice, so they chose December 25th. Although we still don't know the date of Jesus' birth, we know the story. It is in the Bible, our holy book. And we hear it every Christmas.

Luminaria—paper bags with candles and sand inside—light up an ancient Anasazi cliff dwelling in Mesa Verde National Park, Colorado, at Christmastime.

We light candles.

We hear that Jesus was born.

Children in the West Bank town of Bethlehem act out the story of Jesus' birth at the Church of the Nativity. Many Christians believe the church is built on the site of Jesus' birthplace.

We hear that about 2,000 years

ago a woman named Mary was going to have a baby. An angel told her the child would be the Son of God. Mary and her husband, Joseph, traveled to the town of Bethlehem. That's where Jesus was born.

We hear that when Jesus was born a host of angels appeared in the sky and proclaimed, "Peace on Earth." They told nearby shepherds they could find the baby in a stable at an inn in Bethlehem. The shepherds hurried to see Jesus.

We also hear the story of the three wise men, sometimes called the three kings. A star appeared in the night sky and guided these men to Jesus. They brought gifts of gold, frankincense, and myrrh.

Because of the birth of Jesus, Christmas is a time of joy and happiness. We celebrate in many ways, with traditions from many places.

∧ *An Advent wreath*

Some of us get ready for Christmas by observing Advent, which means "coming." We may have an Advent calendar or light candles on an Advent wreath the four Sundays before Christmas.

We think of others.

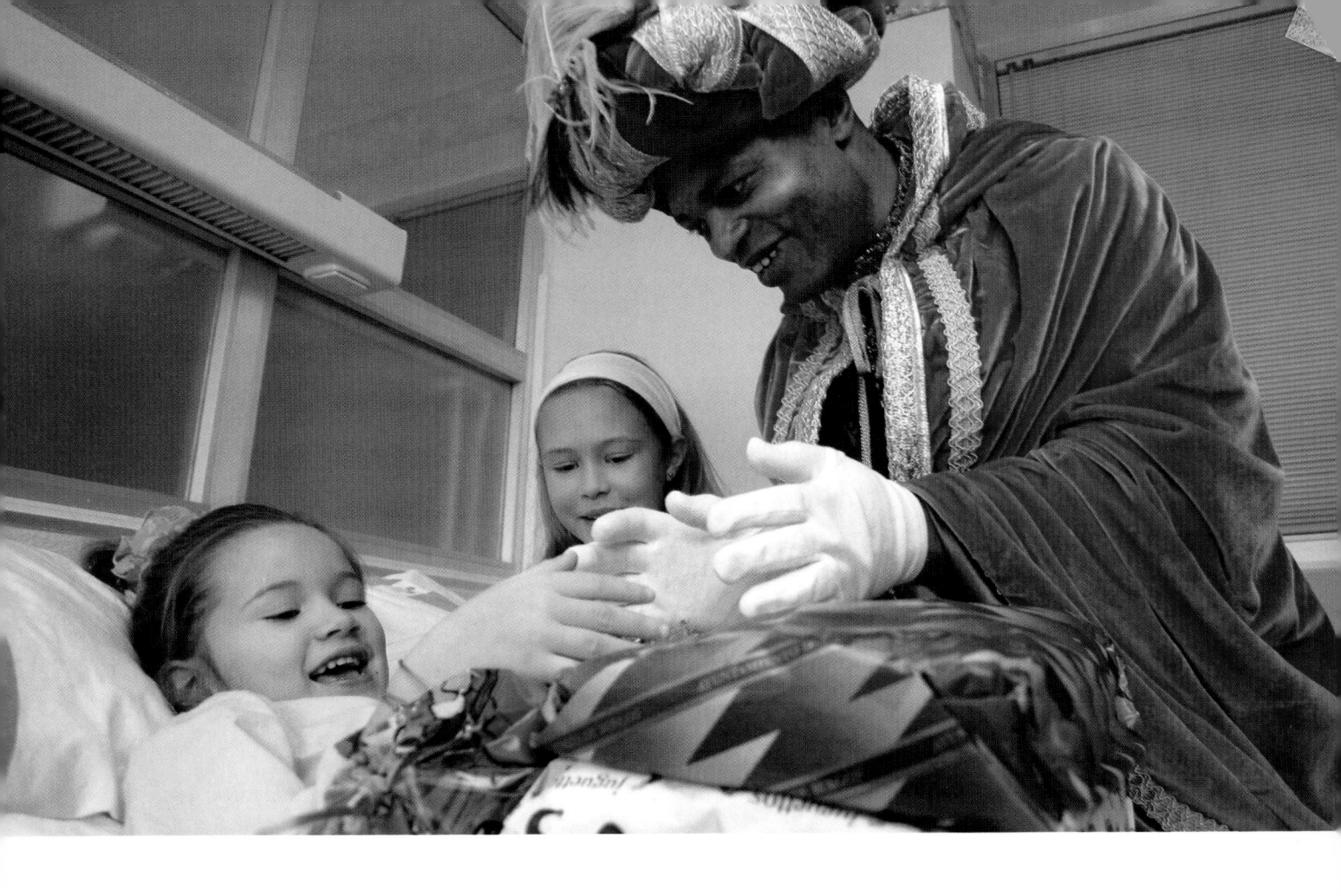

∧ In Spain, a man dressed as one of the three kings gives presents to a girl in a hospital on January 6th, Three Kings Day, which is when many children in Spain get their Christmas presents.

< In Budapest, Hungary, volunteers pack donated toys into gift boxes. The toys will go to children in needy families.

The Christmas season is also a time when we think of others. We give food and gifts to help families who don't have enough money. We volunteer in food kitchens and visit patients in nursing homes and hospitals.

What will you give?

People shop at a Christmas market in Innsbruck, Austria.

∧ *Although Christians are a minority in India, Christmas is celebrated across the country. Here a Muslim girl in Bangalore sells miniature Christmas trees.*

We get ready for Christmas

in other ways, too. We make wish lists of presents we hope we'll get. And we plan what we'll make or buy to give to our friends and family. What will you get this year? What will you give?

∧ *Gingerbread cookies*

We decorate our homes.

We put up wreaths and garlands, holly and mistletoe. We enjoy beautiful poinsettia plants, too. We might even have our own crèche, or nativity scene. We string beautiful Christmas lights outside our homes.

∨ *Berhard Nermerich attaches one more chain of lights in the front yard of his house in Kelsterbach, Germany. This brings the total number of holiday lights at his home to 8,888. It took him and his wife 11 weeks to set up the decorations.*

We decorate.

∧ In Toronto, Canada, Georgia Stewart and her children Brandon, Cheyenne, and Charlize decorate for their first Christmas in their new home.

We spread Christmas cheer. We say, "Merry Christmas!" and "Happy holidays!" We send Christmas cards to friends and family. "May you have a year of joy, a year of peace," we say. We bake cookies and give them to friends and family.

We make our
tree special.

> *Amelia Naegele hangs an ornament on her Christmas tree in Alexandria, Virginia.*

Before Christmas, we get our

tree. The Christmas tree tradition goes back a long, long time. We use an evergreen—a spruce, a fir, or a pine—a tree that stays green all year long. The Christmas tree is a symbol of eternal life.

We make our tree special. We decorate it with ornaments old and new, homemade and bought: glass balls, painted egg shells, Japanese fans, tinkling bells. We drape it with popcorn chains, tinsel, strings of lights. At the very top we put an angel or a star.

< *Rockefeller Center in New York City sparkles at Christmastime.*

15

During the days and nights before

Christmas, we listen to special holiday music. We make music, too. We play instruments and we sing carols. We sing "Silent Night," "Deck the Halls," "Away in a Manger," "We Wish You a Merry Christmas!" We sing in church. We sing with friends. We sing for neighbors. We sing with joy!

We make music.

< On a subway train in Seoul, South Korea, musicians play and sing Christmas carols.

∨ Buddy Hansen and his father, Tim, play in the annual Tuba Christmas concert in Anaheim, California.

< Grace Ivey, Lyndsi Weems, and Isaiah Marcotte sing "Away in a Manger" during Christmas Eve Mass at Sacred Heart Cathedral in Salina, Kansas.

Christmas Eve is a
magical time.

Christmas Eve is December

24th. It is a special, magical time. We hang our stockings. Some of us wait until Christmas Eve to decorate our trees and sing carols. Some of us even give and get presents this evening.

Many people go to church on Christmas Eve. We pray and thank God for Jesus. Some of us go to church for a Candlelight service or Midnight Mass.

And all over the world children go to bed on Christmas Eve waiting for Santa Claus or Saint Nicholas or Kris Kringle or Father Christmas. Snuggled in bed we listen.... Do we hear reindeer bells?

< *Worshippers attend Christmas Eve Mass at a Catholic church in Lalitpur, Nepal.*

What has Santa brought?

∧ *Santa Claus arrives on Waikiki Beach in Honolulu, Hawaii, in an outrigger canoe.*

We've heard that Santa Claus travels from the North Pole all over the world in his flying sleigh pulled by reindeer. In Hawaii, it's said he comes on a boat. In Australia, Santa arrives on water skis. In Ghana, he comes out of the jungle.

20

No matter how he comes, he brings presents! On Christmas morning we look under our tree—what has Santa brought?

Many families go to church on Christmas day. Some of us have special breakfasts. And we cook food for guests who will come later.

∧ A dog dressed in a Santa hat cuddles inside his owner's jacket in Shanghai, China.

< Ellen Sartore surrounds herself with Christmas gifts in her home in Lincoln, Nebraska.

Christmas dinner!

> A Yule log

< Children, parents, and grandparents from a Mexican-American family make tamales for Christmas dinner in Torrance, California.

v A family in Richmond, Virginia, enjoys being together for Christmas dinner.

On Christmas we celebrate with

our family and our friends. We sit down together for a delicious Christmas dinner. We have turkey, ham, roast pork, goose, gingerbread, plum pudding, mince pie, a Yule log cake, fruitcake. We drink egg nog, cider, hot chocolate. Some of us also eat rice and beans, tamales, oyster stuffing, lutefisk, dumplings, or ravioli.

Christmas is a time to celebrate the birth of Jesus Christ. It is a time to spread joy and love. Christmas is a time for peace on earth, good will to all. We pray for peace everywhere.

People in Mountainside, New Jersey, gather together for the annual Christmas tree lighting.

Good will to all.

MORE ABOUT CHRISTMAS

Contents

Just the Facts

WHO CELEBRATES IT: Christians. Many people celebrate the non-religious aspects of Christmas.

WHAT IT IS: A joyful holiday that celebrates the birth of Jesus Christ.

WHEN: Most people celebrate Christmas on December 24th and 25th. People in many countries, particularly Eastern Orthodox Christians, exchange gifts on January 6th, the Epiphany, which celebrates the arrival of the wise men after their long journey from the East.

HOW LONG: Christmas itself is one day, beginning on Christmas Eve and lasting until Christmas night. Some people observe Advent for the month leading up to Christmas. The Twelve Days of Christmas are from Christmas night (December 25th) to the morning of January 6th, the Epiphany, when the three wise men came to give Jesus gifts.

RITUALS: Praying, caroling, acting out the Nativity, giving presents, helping the needy.

FOOD: Cookies, candy canes, egg nog, Yule log cake, Christmas dinner.

Memory Books

My friend Julie started this tradition with her family.

1. Make or buy little notebooks or blank books that are about two inches square. Each person in the family should have a book. The books should have enough pages to last for several years.

2. Gather your family together around the Christmas tree. Put your name on the front of your book. You can decorate it, too, if you like.

3. Write the year on the first page of the book.

4. Turn the page and answer this question: *What was something you did for the first time since last Christmas?*

5. Turn the page and answer this question: *What was your favorite moment of the year?*

6. Turn the page andcomplete this sentence: *By next Christmas I hope to _____.*

7. Together as a family, make up some of your own questions. Think about big goals and wishes. For example you could write: *If I knew I couldn't fail, I would _____.* Or: *If I could do one thing to make the world a better place, I would _____.*

8. When you're done, put next year's date at the top of the next page. Now the book is ready for next Christmas.

9. Hang your book on the tree by winding a string around it and attaching a paper clip to the end of the string.

Three Kings Day

At the end of the Twelve Days of Christmas comes a special day called the Epiphany, or Three Kings Day. This holiday, which falls on January 6th, is celebrated as the day when the three wise men, also called the three kings, first saw baby Jesus and gave him gifts. The Epiphany is celebrated in different ways around the world.

Children in Puerto Rico go to sleep on January 5th with anticipation, for the next morning they will get presents. Before they go to sleep they leave a box with hay under their beds. The hay is for the three kings' camels—so the kings will leave good presents. In Mexico, Spain, and Argentina, children leave their shoes out for the kings to fill with presents. They also leave wine, fruit, milk, and cookies for the kings and their camels.

In France, a special "king cake" is baked for Three Kings Day. The baker hides a coin, jewel, or little toy inside it. Whoever gets the piece of cake with the trinket inside gets to be king for a day. In New Orleans, Louisiana, which was settled by the French, king cakes are a special treat marking the beginning of the Carnival season, which starts on the Epiphany and ends on Mardi Gras, a carnival celebration on Fat Tuesday, the day before Lent begins.

In addition to celebrating the visit of the three kings, on the Epiphany, people in the Eastern Orthodox Church also remember Jesus' baptism in the River Jordan and his first miracle, when he turned water into wine. In Tarpon Springs, Florida, there is a famous Greek Orthodox celebration every year on the Epiphany. A priest blesses the water and the boats. Then a cross is thrown into the chilly waters of the Spring Bayou. Brave people dive in after it, and whoever gets the cross is said to be blessed for the whole year.

< *Sixteen-year-old Jack Vasilaros comes up with the cross during the 2006 Epiphany celebration in Tarpon Springs, Florida.*

Swallow Family Christmas Cake

My friend Pamela Curtis Swallow gave me this delicious recipe. She says you can double it and bake it in a larger pan (13-by-9 inches).

INGREDIENTS FOR THE CAKE:
1 1/2 tablespoons butter, softened
1/2 cup sugar
1/4 cup evaporated milk
1/4 cup water
1 cup flour
1/2 teaspoon salt
1 teaspoon baking soda
1 cup fresh cranberries

INGREDIENTS FOR THE SAUCE:
1/4 pound (1 stick) butter
1 cup sugar
1/2 cup evaporated milk
1 teaspoon vanilla

YOU WILL ALSO NEED:
An 8-by-8-inch pan
Butter and flour for the pan
An electric mixer, if possible

Ask an adult to help you.

1. Preheat oven to 350°F.

2. Butter and flour the pan.

3. In a large bowl, cream 1 1/2 tablespoons butter and 1/2 cup sugar with the mixer.

4. Combine 1/4 cup evaporated milk and 1/4 cup water in a glass measuring cup or a bowl with a spout.

5. Sift together flour, salt, and baking soda into a small bowl.

6. Using the mixer, add milk-and-water combination to butter-and-sugar mixture alternately with sifted dry ingredients.

7. Using a spoon, fold cranberries into batter. (Do not use the electric mixer for this.) The batter will be thin.

8. Pour batter into prepared pan.

9. Bake for 30 minutes at 350°F.

10. Test for doneness by inserting a toothpick into the cake's center. If it's still gooey, bake a few more minutes, then test again.

11. When the cake is done, make the sauce by bringing all the sauce ingredients to a boil for two minutes in a saucepan on the stove, stirring constantly. (You don't want it to burn or boil over, so be careful!)

12. Cut cake into squares. Just before serving, pour warm sauce on each serving of cake.

Find Out More

BOOKS

Those with a star (*) are especially good for children.

*Barth, Edna. *Holly, Reindeer, and Colored Lights: The Story of the Christmas Symbols.* Illustrated by Ursula Arndt. Clarion Books, 2000. This is a really good book for older children interested in learning more about the history of Christmas symbols.

*Lankford, Mary D. *Christmas Around the World.* Illustrated by Karen Dugan. Morrow Junior Books, 1995. This book explains how 12 different countries, including the United States, celebrate Christmas. It also has Christmas sayings, crafts, and some historical facts.

*Pfeffer, Wendy. *The Shortest Day: Celebrating the Winter Solstice.* Illustrated by Jesse Reisch. Dutton Children's Books, 2003. This wonderful book tells all about the solstice—historically, scientifically, and socially.

Pleck, Elizabeth. *Celebrating the Family: Ethnicity, Consumer Culture, and Family Rituals.* Harvard University Press, 2000. Chapter three is a terrific look at the history and sociology of Christmas in the United States.

Santino, Jack. *All Around the Year: Holidays and Celebrations in American Life.* University of Illinois Press, 1994. Chapter five includes a fascinating discussion of the origins of Christmas customs and traditions.

*Winthrop, Elizabeth. *The First Christmas Stocking.* Delacorte, 2006. A fictional recounting of how stockings came to be hung by the hearth and filled with gifts at Christmas.

WEB SITES

There are many Web sites about Christmas. Here are two of my favorites.

http://www.worldofchristmas.net This is a very extensive Web site about Christmas. It has history, traditions, recipes, etc.

http://www.howstuffworks.com/christmas.htm This site will answer a lot of your Christmas questions.

∨ *In Puri, India, a 100-foot-long Santa Claus sand sculpture by artist Sudarshan Pattnalk attracts admirers.*

Glossary

Advent (AD-vent): The period of time beginning four Sundays before Christmas when Christians look forward to the anniversary of the coming of Jesus Christ into the world.

Crèche (KRESH): A model of the baby Jesus surrounded by his parents, visitors, and animals in the stable (or cave) where he was born.

Frankincense (FRANK-in-sense): Part of a tree that gives off a pleasant scent when burned; a kind of incense.

Lutefisk (LUTE-fisk): A fish dish from Norway and Sweden.

Myrrh (MEHR): A nice-smelling, sticky plant substance used in incense and perfume.

Nativity (nay-TIV-uh-tee): The birth of Jesus; also a display or scene showing it.

Solstice (SOLE-stis): The winter solstice is the shortest day—and longest night—of the year. The summer solstice is the longest day—and shortest night—of the year. In the Northern Hemisphere, the winter solstice occurs on December 21 or 22 and the summer solstice on June 21 or 22. In the Southern Hemisphere, the seasons are reversed: The winter solstice is in June, the summer solstice in December.

Where This Book's Photos Were Taken

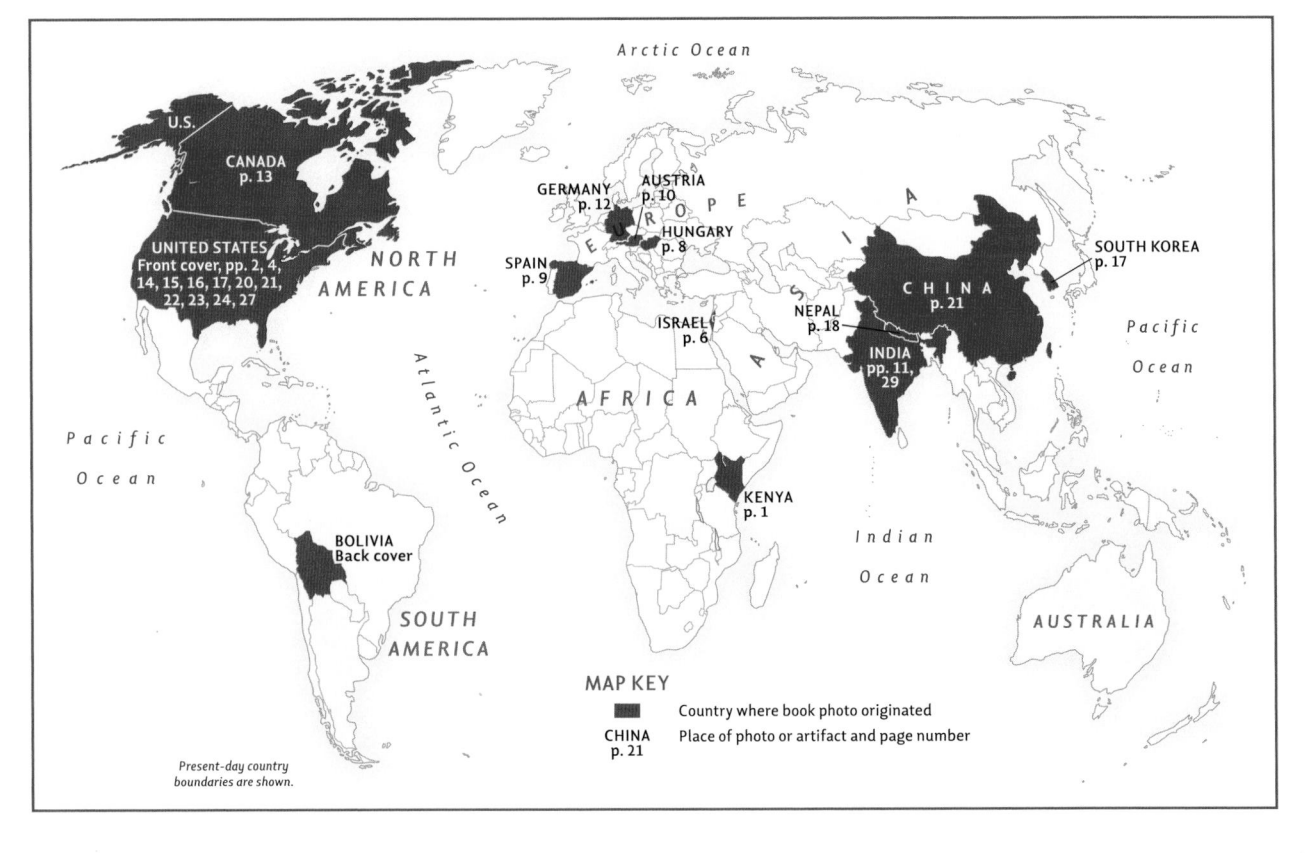

Christmas: Celebrating the Good News

By the Reverend Nathan Humphrey

When I was a child, my mother would place a label that she made with glitter and glue on each of our Christmas presents. There, sparkling up at us, was a reminder: "John 3:16." This Bible verse is perhaps the most succinct statement of the good news about Jesus' birth: "For God so loved the world that he gave his only begotten Son, that whosoever believeth in him should not perish, but have everlasting life." *

My mother wanted us to remember that Christmas wasn't just about the presents that were bought in stores, but about the most priceless gift of all: God's love, incarnate in Jesus Christ. We exchange gifts so that we might be reminded of *that* gift. The contemporary commercialism and consumerism of Christmas tend to overshadow this central aspect of the holiday.

No one knows the day of Jesus' real birthday, though we do know that he was born over 2,000 years ago. Christians didn't begin celebrating Christmas on December 25th until A.D. 336, in Rome. Most of the traditions Christians observe at Christmas are derived from the Gospel according to St. Luke: the inn, the manger, the shepherds, the angels. But another story, from St. Matthew's Gospel, has been interwoven: that of the star and the Magi, also known as the Wise Men or Three Kings. Matthew likely intended this story to be understood as happening some time after Jesus' birth. (It would have taken the Magi a while to travel to Bethlehem after observing the star!)

While most of us are happy to combine the two stories into one event, many Christians, particularly from the Eastern Orthodox tradition, give great precedence to the visit of the Magi by remembering their visit on the Epiphany, a Greek word meaning "manifestation" or "appearance." The Orthodox exchange gifts on this day, not on Christmas, since it was on the Epiphany that the Magi presented their gifts of gold, frankincense, and myrrh to Jesus.

On the Epiphany, many Christians also remember two other manifestations of God in Christ: Jesus' baptism in the Jordan River and his first miracle of turning water into wine at a wedding at Cana in Galilee. The Epiphany is celebrated 12 days after Christmas—hence the famous carol beginning, "On the first day of Christmas/ my true love gave to me/ a partridge in a pear tree…" and continuing through the Twelfth Day. In the days of Shakespeare, Epiphany Eve, or Twelfth Night (also the name of one of his plays), marked the end of Christmas festivities.

Although few people have the leisure to stretch out their Christmas merrymaking over 12 days anymore, our culture has tended to divide Christmas itself into two distinct holidays. The first one is religious, centered on the remembrance of Jesus' birth. We rejoice in the re-telling of the tale of a God who loved us so much that this God came to dwell with us, to live and die as one of us, to reconcile us to the God and Father of us all. The second Christmas holiday is secular, centered on giving—and getting—gifts. To this latter holiday belong many of the outward trappings of the season: Santa Claus and Christmas trees and festive holiday displays in front yards and shop windows. Christmas celebrated as a purely secular holiday, however, can leave many of us feeling hollow and lonely, particularly when we realize that *things* can never take the place of *people*, and it is only through relationships that we discover that Divine spark of love that Christ's birth reveals in all its glory.

This Christmas, and every Christmas, I wish you and yours every blessing. May this book enrich your appreciation of this unique holiday and enliven your celebration of it.

Nathan Humphrey

The Reverend Nathan Humphrey is a priest of St. Paul's Parish, K Street, the Episcopal Diocese of Washington, D.C. He is a graduate of Yale Divinity School and St. John's College, Annapolis, MD.

* Quotation is from the King James Version of the Bible.

For Julie

PICTURE CREDITS

Front cover: © Phoebe Dunn/Stock Connection/ipnStock.com; Back cover: © David Mercado/Corbis; Spine: © Danilo Ducak/Shutterstock; 1: © Sayyid Azim/Associated Press; 2: © Lisa Romerein/Botanica/Jupiter Images; 3 up: © Katrina Brown/Shutterstock; 3 lo: © Christopher Ewing/Shutterstock; 4-5: © Ira Block/NG Image Collection; 6-7: © Kevin Frayer/Associated Press; 8 up: © Thomas Northcut/Getty Images; 8 lo: © Rafiq Maqbool/Associated Press; 9: © Felix Ordonez Ausin/Reuters/Corbis; 10: © Fantuz Olimpio/eStock Photo; 11: © Jagadeesh Nv/Reuters/Corbis; 12 up: © Photodisc; 12 lo: © Frank Rumpenhorst/epa/Corbis; 13: © Tony Bock/Toronto Star/ZUMA Press; 14: © J. B. Grant/eStock Photo; 15: © Mary T. Naegele; 16 up: © Brian Cahn/WpN; 16 lo: © Ryan Soderlin/Salina Journal/Associated Press; 17: © Lee Jin-man/Associated Press; 18-19: © Narendra Shrestha/EPA; 20 up: © Color China Photo/Associated Press; 20 lo: © Joel Sartore /NG Image Collection; 21: © Lucy Pemoni/Reuters/Corbis; 22 up: © Kayte M. Deioma/PhotoEdit Inc.; 22 lo: © Albert Barr/Shutterstock; 23: © Ariel Skelley/Corbis; 24-25: © Tony Kurdzuk/The Star-Ledger/Corbis; 27: © Carrie Pratt/Pool Photo/St. Petersburg Times/WpN; 28: © Elizabeth Watt Photography/Stockfood; 29: © epa/Corbis.

Text copyright © 2007 Deborah Heiligman

Library of Congress Cataloging-in-Publication Data

Heiligman, Deborah.
   Celebrate Christmas / Deborah Heiligman ; consultant, The Reverend Nathan J.A. Humphrey.
      p. cm. — (Holidays around the world)
   Includes bibliographical references and index.
   ISBN 978-1-4263-0122-3 (trade : alk. paper)
   ISBN 978-1-4263-0123-0 (library : alk. paper)
   I. Christmas—Juvenile literature. I. Humphrey, Nathan J. A.
II. Title.
BV45.H425 2007
263'.915—dc22
                          2007012659
Printed in the United States of America

Front cover: A boy drags a freshly cut Christmas tree through snow-covered woods in Connecticut. *Back cover:* A girl in La Paz, Bolivia, gazes at ornaments showing a Nativity scene. *Title page:* A girl in Nairobi, Kenya, prays at a candlelight service on Christmas Eve.

Founded in 1888, the National Geographic Society is one of the largest nonprofit scientific and educational organizations in the world. It reaches more than 285 million people worldwide each month through its official journal, NATIONAL GEOGRAPHIC, and its four other magazines; the National Geographic Channel; television documentaries; radio programs; films; books; videos and DVDs; maps; and interactive media. National Geographic has funded more than 8,000 scientific research projects and supports an education program combating geographic illiteracy.

For more information, please call 1-800-NGS LINE (647-5463) or write to the following address:

National Geographic Society
1145 17th Street N.W., Washington, D.C. 20036-4688 U.S.A.

Visit us online at www.nationalgeographic.com/books

For information about special discounts for bulk purchases, please contact National Geographic Books Special Sales: ngspecsales@ngs.org

Published by the National Geographic Society.
John M. Fahey, Jr., *President and Chief Executive Officer*
Gilbert M. Grosvenor, *Chairman of the Board*
Nina D. Hoffman, *Executive Vice President; President, Book Publishing Group*

STAFF FOR THIS BOOK

Nancy Laties Feresten, *Vice President, Editor-in-Chief of Children's Books*
Bea Jackson, *Design and Illustrations Director, Children's Books*
Amy Shields, *Executive Editor, Children's Books*
Marfé Ferguson Delano, *Project Editor*
Lori Epstein, *Illustrations Editor*
Melissa Brown, *Project Designer*
Carl Mehler, *Director of Maps*
Priyanka Lamichhane, *Assistant Editor*
Rebecca Baines, *Release Editor*
Jennifer A. Thornton, *Managing Editor*
Gary Colbert, *Production Director*
Lewis R. Bassford, *Production Manager*
Maryclare Tracy, Nicole Elliott, *Manufacturing Managers*

Series design by 3+Co. and Jim Hiscott.
The body text in the book is set in Mrs. Eaves.
The display text is Lisboa.

ACKNOWLEDGMENTS

Thanks to The Reverend Nathan Humphrey for his great counsel at a very busy time. (Welcome to the world baby Margaret!) Thanks to Pat Brisson for invaluable input and to Pamela Curtis Swallow for her cake recipe and welcome interference. (Though I'd like to note that it turns out this Christmas cake is also a much-loved tradition in Nathan Humphrey's family!) Marfé Ferguson Delano and Lori Epstein were, as always, tireless in making this book the best it could be. And Becky Baines for helping to put it to bed. Nancy Feresten heads the whole crew, and she deserves thanks, kudos, and a vacation in a tropical isle somewhere. Last but not least, thanks to Julie Stockler, to whom this book is dedicated. I can always count on her for support, fashion advice, perspective, and most importantly, a good laugh. Julie, I hope people across the world take up your little book tradition. I'm bowing out now...Happy holidays!